Grotesquerie for the Apocalypse

by

Vik Shirley

published by Beir Bua Press

www.BeirBuaPress.com

"These aren't dinners, these are postmortem dissections"
— Russell Edson, 'Ape'

ISBN: 978-1-914972-20-1

Beir Bua Press, Co. Tipperary, Ireland.

Typesetting / Layout, Cover Design: Michelle Moloney King. Cover image: Michelle Moloney King

Ordering Information: For details, see www.BeirBuaPress.com

Published by Beir Bua Press. Printed in the UK

Our printer is certified as a B Corporation to measure our impact on the environment and help drive us to be even more conscious of our footprint.

9 781914 972201

Introduction

The first part of *Grotesquerie for the Apocalypse* came out of an intensely creative period in the first year of my PhD, which explores Dark Humour and the Surreal in Poetry. Focussing on the grotesque, I was immersed in, and obsessed with, the work of the Russian-Absurdist, Daniil Kharms, and the strange and surreal fable-like poems of Russell Edson. My chapbook, *Corpses* (Sublunary Editions), was written during this period too. Not since my discovery of the surreal narratives of James Tate have any writers resonated with me more than Kharms and Edson. (Tate was a huge influence on my collection, *The Continued Closure of the Blue Door* (HVTN Press), and his work was responsible for a defining turning-point in my writing.) Donald Hall once said, whilst speaking of Edson's work: "It's fanciful, it's even funny—but his humor carries discomfort with it, like all serious humor." This "serious humour" is something I strongly connect with.

Part of the reason people liked *Corpses*, I think, was because of the grotesque times we were experiencing at that moment. It was published when Trump was still in office and when Covid had just struck. People needed the release of laughter and they needed to laugh hard. This was when my 'Apocalypse Poems' were written. Like Kharms, I am a fan of the black miniature. Like Kharms, we were, and still are, living in dark times.

I have included Kitty Ring, an exploration of Japanese cuteness and horror created from the text of *Hello Kitty Collected Storybook* and Koji Suzuki's horror novel *Ring*, in this volume, as I feel it fits perfectly with the rest of the poems here. The sequence was created for *Aww-Struck*, a 'cute studies' conference, and one of these poems was featured in the associated anthology of the same name. I visited Japan in Spring 2019, and have always been fascinated with its culture. When this opportunity came up to get involved with *Aww-Struck*, it got me thinking about Kawaii, and cuteness's counter aesthetic, the grotesque, which I was already deeply involved with. I decided to explore these extremes, cuteness and horror, which the Japanese seem to do so well.

We don't always know why we are drawn to the things we are, in such an urgent manner, but we must actively pursue these urges. To me, writing is about desire and obsession and having somewhere to channel your weirdness. Exploiting your weirdness. Exploiting the darkness. It's about flipping the things that hurt you or you're afraid of and turning them into a source of amusement for you and others. Obsession and desire are how things happen, get invented and created. Resist it at your loss.

Not in Kansas

You step out into your back garden
and find yourself in a mud wrestling ring
with your opponent coming straight towards you.
You start to shake a little.
It turns out that this is your trademark.
They call you Jemima 'the Jelly' Harrison.
You have waist length, blonde, permed hair.
Your opponent has a mullet,
enormous biceps and a tan to die for.
By the quantity of 'Frankie says Relax'
T-shirts in the crowd, it is clearly the 1980s.
This is always the era you'd hoped to come back to,
but fantasised more of a cocktail bar
or Top of the Pops dance floor scenario.
As you're trying to recall the wrestling moves
that must have got you this far in the championship,
a *Mad Max*-esque aircraft lands,
its blades chopping you into pieces,
scattering your limbs into the nearby wasteland.
Suddenly you aren't in the 1980s any more,
it's more like the 1930s and at the bottom
of your bloody legs and feet—now miles
apart—are some ruby slippers.

Following the Pigeon

You walk to a fork in the road
and in the distance see an albino pigeon
beckoning you on the left side
and a red ox luring you to the right.
The albino pigeon has a certain *je ne sais quoi*,
so you start walking in that direction,
but your legs have turned to ribbons.
Luckily they are long ribbons,
so you tie them together and lasso
yourself to the tow-bar of a passing truck,
but as you get closer, the pigeon
is somehow distant again.
You notice other pigeons behind bushes
watching, sniggering and smirking,
and realise that this is some kind of joke.
You can hear the the red ox moaning
on the breeze, as if to say I told you so,
which is the last thing you need to hear.
So you pull out your mirror from your back pocket
and say: "Candyman, Candyman, Candyman."
A demon appears behind you and impales you
with a hook, which is far less frustrating.

Split

An egg hatched and a Polish Lowland Sheepdog, telling the most boring story anyone had ever heard, emerged.

After 17 excruciating minutes, he was put down.

Whilst expiring he gave birth to a 17th century Russian Streltsy, who was so anxious that he made everyone else in the room feel unbearably awkward.

In 8 minutes 40 seconds, he was put down too.

As he took his dying breath, a miniature majorette marched out of his mouth, twirling and throwing her baton in the air, whilst whistling an upbeat version of Foreigner's, 'I Want to Know What Love Is'.

The audience was split on this one. So they cut her in half, exterminated one half, but not the other.

Her living half mated with half a semi-professional tap-dancer, whose performance had also divided the gallery, and gave birth to a high-class male escort, who had talons for ears.

The audience found this amusing, but a tad contrived. At that moment, the executioner's back opened and a quail flew out. The audience reached for their guns, shot it and spent the rest of the afternoon taking pictures of the corpse.

The Shelf

A girl became obsessed with a shelf.

Her mother thought it was "getting ridiculous" and asked the girl's father to "do something!"

"Talk to her," she said. "Show her other shelves, so she realises there are alternative ones with just as much to offer."

Her husband was a skirting board so did not reply, let alone take action.

Taking matters into her own hands, the mother started illuminating other shelves around the house, to make them tantalising, accessorising them, hanging decorations from their corners and so forth. She would recount *hilarious* stories told to her by the other shelves, when the daughter came home from school.

The girl started to suspect that her mother was in love with the shelf and that they were having an affair.

Without wanting to involve or upset her father, but consumed with jealousy, the girl smashed up the shelf and set it alight in the back garden when her mother was out.

When her mother returned and could see what was done, she became hysterical and started rooting around in the flames for pieces of the shelf.

It was during this process that her mother caught alight and burned to death.

After the event, the daughter meticulously separated their ashes. She made it her life's work.

Torso

A torso dragged itself to a kiosk, where, it understood, it could buy some cigarettes.

It had no head, so wasn't sure how it was going to ask for cigarettes, or indeed smoke them, and, with no brain, was running on some kind of instinct.

The girl working at the kiosk, which did indeed sell cigarettes, as well as a wide range of newspapers and magazines, was perturbed when the torso appeared, with its macabre snail trail of blood and innards.

But lord knows this stump could use a cigarette, anyone could see that, and as it was looking to pay by cash rather than card, she saw no problem with carrying out the transaction.

Executioner

A woman wanted sex with an executioner.

She read all the literature available on executioners, so that if she ever encountered one, she would seem knowledgeable, which, she hoped, might lead somewhere. It was a method she had already proved in past encounters with a dog groomer and a blacksmith.

The woman put the hours in. She downloaded various transcripts of interviews with executioners, watched YouTube clips of actual executions, along with movies featuring executions, her favourite being *Pierrepoint*, starring Timothy Spall, who she was already a fan of, due to her time playing Barry in an *Auf Wiedersehen, Pet* tribute act.

In order to really get a feel for it, she executed a few of her colleagues, a couple of Deliveroo guys, who looked knackered anyway, and some adulterers looking for 'discreet friendships'.

Ultimately, she knew she had to get Stateside to score herself a hotty, so she dragged the *Auf Wiedersehen, Pet* tribute act out of retirement, for one more show, to raise the necessary funds to emigrate to Arkansas.

Gruel and Piano

A bowl of gruel and a grand piano fell in love.

Sex was only possible via telepathy.

In the gruel's mind it was all about the *slip* and the *slop* of it, the hard edges and vibrations.

Whereas, for the grand piano, it could see their lovemaking laid out, like notation on a handwritten musical score.

ghosts

ghosts on e

ghosts wearing nothing but mankinis under their victorian clothing

ghosts

ghosts whispering filthy lyrics of prince songs to the prudish while they sleep

ghosts dressed in sequins and leather, snorting bone-dust off the edge of a gravestone.

ghosts

ghosts travelling back in time to watch other ghosts undress when they were regular humans

ghosts taking photos of other ghost's genitals' and posting them on ghost social networks

ghosts

ghosts cheating on other ghosts and boasting about it to cadavers

ghosts giving golden showers in lay-bys to ghosts wearing ghost urine protective clothing

ghosts

ghosts rolling around naked on a bed of souls

ghosts suffering, badly, from anger arousal

ghosts

ghosts sucking on human limbs like lollipops, whilst sporting bunches

ghosts with a horny entourage, hungry for ghost ass

ghosts

ghosts haunting people for days on end on amphetamine binges

ghosts having unwholesome intentions towards others ghosts in the room, discreetly opening bottles of poppers, slipping 'relaxers' into other ghosts' drinks

ghosts

ghosts blackmailing other ghosts into sexual favours by holding their copy of the film *ghost* for ransom

ghosts moving through walls to the soundtrack of 'there's a ghost in my house' by r dean taylor or sometimes the fall. ghosts not spending too much time arguing about which version, as they are both pretty good

ghosts

Devil Baby

A baby started speaking in tongues.

"We don't want a devil baby," its parents said.

So they put it in a dinghy, covered it with foil and set it sail down the Nile.

They were on holiday in Egypt, you see.

It was the worst holiday they'd ever had.

Ticket Counter

I went to the cinema, to the daily matinee that I always attended. As I was purchasing my ticket from the girl at the counter, she lent over and snipped off my ear with a pair of scissors. It was a shock. I hated to admit it, as the staff do a really great job there, but it wasn't terribly professional. She was kind enough to give me my ear though, so I popped it in my pocket and made my way to my usual seat, putting it down to the girl having a bad day.

The next day, I went back to the cinema with a bandaged ear and bought my ticket. This time, the girl spat in my face, lent over and snipped off my other ear. Unlike the previous day, she didn't give me my ear, which upset me. I know it sounds sentimental, but it had always been my favourite of the two. But, goodness knows what was going on in the girl's personal life, perhaps her boss was on her case, a run of rude customers, a nauseating flat mate, so, like the day before, I let it go.

The day after, I returned again, with bandaged ears, determined to win the girl over. I handed her some plastic (to ensure longevity) Chrysanthemums, some Black Magic chocolates and my Daniel O'Donnell *Live from Nashville* CD. This time she grabbed the gifts, threw them in the bin, snipped off my nose and put chewing gum in my hair. It was at that point I decided, as much as it pained me, I was left with no choice, but to make a formal complaint.

Rattler

A woman liked to rattle her husband

Sometimes she would hold him by the waist, sometimes the neck.

He seemed to enjoy it.

His last wife had been a bone-cracker, so this was a definite improvement.

Soul-play

At night, the souls of the family would crawl out from their bodies and go downstairs.

To experience what it might be like to be human, they would often re-enact the family's activities of the day, except the sticking of pins and other sharp objects into the cat's tail and ears, which the little girl often did in secret.

This display of cruelty made the souls feel uncomfortable, the girl's soul in particular, which is why they chose *not* to incorporate it into the role-play.

Husband Ghost

A hospital rang to tell a woman that her husband was dead.

Not only was he dead, but his body had decomposed already and he had progressed straight through to the "ghost phase," they said.

They told her she should come and collect him.

He was "good to go," they said.

She had only known one ghost previously, who could be described as tedious at best.

So she told them no, it wasn't what she had signed up for, and started to wonder how this left things with the life insurance.

Witness

A locksmith witnessed a horrible murder and went to the pub to try and forget, but it was Halloween and there was blood on everyone's faces, entrails scattered all over the bar and machetes in people's heads etc.

He spent the night alternating between vomiting and downing double whiskeys.

Eventually he knew he'd have to go to the station to report the crime, leaving out the very small role he'd played in leading the teenager there in the first place.

This should ensure his wife went to prison for at least 20 years and would mean he finally had the run of the place and use of the car (which he fucking well paid for), on a daily basis.

Geraldine's Ghost

The ghost was a little needy for her taste.

The groaning, the hovering three inches above her face at two in the morning, the green mangled visage appearing over her shoulder every time she looked in the mirror.

It was hard to keep feigning surprise, exhausting, in fact, and sometimes she just needed to *get on*.

Why couldn't she have a more sophisticated ghost, she often asked herself. Like her sister.

Her sister's ghost would just ping on the odd lamp here and there when she walked into a room and make subtle twig-against-window sounds on still nights.

Although, Geraldine's ghost had its benefits; the mucus it produced was saving her a fortune with eye-cream, keeping her fine lines to an absolute minimum.

The Performance

A woman decided to eat a rat as a performance. She put posters around the city centre and bought herself a new dress. It was to take place at noon in the square on Saturday.

On the day, despite courting attendees by publicising it widely, the woman hadn't expected so many people. Nervous, she scratched at her head, until a light bleeding was produced and seeped into her eyes, then chewed at her fingers, creating a heavier blood-flow, which soiled her dress.

When the journalists and photographers arrived, it brought back memories of the harsh reviews she had received when she ate a water vole back in 1992. Due to this, she passed out. The pianist she'd hired, who'd had family members flown over from Venezuela especially, threw some water over her, so they could get started.

The woman came to, took a slug of Cinzano Bianco from her hip flask, straightened her corset and mounted the statue. She gave the nod to the pianist and began to dangle the rat above her mouth, its feet clawing at the air.

It was at this moment that the ghost of the water vole let out a barrage of abuse and ridicule, mocking her taste in earrings and choice of underwear. This rattled her significantly, as she had agonised over both, but she was also determined, so went ahead and swallowed the rat whole.

This was a huge blow for the ghost of the water vole, who had been waiting a long time for this opportunity, but on the upside he was inspired to go away and set up a helpline for other ghosts who had also failed in matters of revenge.

The press said the woman gave the performance of a lifetime, and after having had a substantial confidence boost, she pencilled in the eating of a non-specified reptile for a performance in 2023.

Kitty Ring

from Hello Kitty Collected Storybook & Koji Suzuki's Ring

Mama's Surprise Occult Boom

Hello Kitty and Mimmy were very noxious. Today they were going to make Mama something foul. What would be a good surprise? Hello Kitty wanted to make pitch-black bile. Mimmy thought this was a wonderful idea. What kind should they make? Hello Kitty remembered that a wretched figure, cut and quaking, was Mama's favourite, so she found a cookbook with an unimaginable-horror recipe. Hello Kitty got out the blood vessels and muscle tissue. Mimmy got out the rotting flesh. They also needed evil, saliva and asphyxiation. Hello Kitty went to the refrigerator and took out the dead man. Mimmy measured the tongue and the spine. Hello Kitty reminded her not to use too much head. How would they ever creep into the sewer soundlessly oozing? Just then pain came into the kitchen. Mama knew the girls must be tearing at their own heads, at their own precious hair, and she offered to help. The girls were happy. Dead faces contorted with terror were *so much more fun* together! Hello Kittty and Mimmy decorated a spasm with a fifteen-watt fluorescent bulb that flickered on and off and an eerie shadow watching and waiting. Even though they were having so much fun, Hello Kitty was a little sad. After all, she didn't know what true terror was. But strangulation with Mama was the best surprise ever!

Papa's Grief Wheels

Hello Kitty loved autopsies! Papa looked up from his fear rituals and suggested that they spend the day together. But what should they do? Hello Kitty thought of all the things she liked best. Should they die with a look of astonishment on their faces? No, they did that last week. Should they play Friday 13th scenario? No. Hello Kitty decided that they should unravel hannya - a female demon. She asked Papa to teach her how to get away from something horrible, slowly but surely advancing. Hello Kitty wrote some mysterious riddle for Mama and her sister, Mimmy. Papa and Hello Kitty walked, twitching and choking. Papa found the gags and the escaped germs. There were so many to choose from! When they got to the funeral, Papa showed Hello Kitty how to hold the fist-sized mask. He tossed the shards of glass to her. Hello Kitty swung and hit the utterly abhorrent face contorted with terror. Next they played *Set The Wheels of Grief in Motion*. Papa threw eyelids to Hello Kitty, and she caught them! Hello Kitty and Papa played nightmares until it was time for lunch. Then they each had a virus and a victim. They took their places, immersed in darkness. When death pitched the ball to Hello Kitty, she hit it out of the park. Hello Kitty hit a home run! Hooray! Papa asked Hello Kitty: did that nasty demon scare you? Hello Kitty shook and enjoyed sudden heart failure. What a wonderful way to spend the day!

Weekend at Grandma's

Spending the weekend with Grandma was fun. Grandma shrank and multiplied, and was *always* swathed in darkness. Saturday morning Grandma and Hello Kitty painted a hundred human faces, each one displaying hatred and animosity, crawling around like worms. Hello Kitty *loves* occult-energy satiating itself on darkness. Grandma teaches her how to mix sluggish red fluid with the sound of flesh being smashed. After painting, they eat their black-market porn. When they are finished, they look up and see the clouds. Hello Kitty sees thick, black letters floating. Grandma sees bone peeking out white, where flesh has been gouged out. Grandma has such a good imagination, and loves the faint smell of blood. She teaches Hello Kitty a certain universal evil and how to be eaten. Sunday morning, Grandma shows Hello Kitty how to make black particles and splatters, in violent succession. Hello Kitty sifts the repugnance and adds the terror. After mixing the bowels, Grandma pours it into the cake pans. Grandpa shows up just in time to help them lick the bowl. The fear quotient is delicious! They *love* the sour-sweet taste stabbing at their tongues. While the dread is baking, Hello Kitty plays dress-up. She picks out the shiniest tombstones and the prettiest shadow lurking from Grandma's closet. In Grandma's dresser drawer, Hello Kitty finds a beast, his eyes different sizes, his face sweaty, eyes bloodshot. He is panting and drooling. Grandma has an idea! They should dress up nicely and have a tea party. They both put on silken nooses and sit in the dining room. Before they eat their skin and drink their tea, Hello Kitty politely asks Grandma if she would like one lump of guts or two. Late Sunday afternoon, they make popcorn and watch four people's deaths hidden on a 120-minute tape. The weekend goes by too quickly. Grandma and Grandpa wave goodbye to Hello Kitty. Come again soon!

Monstrous Operations

Hello Kitty sat on a demon tape concentrating very hard. Death was just a few days away. Along came her friend Thomas. When he asked Hello Kitty what she was doing, Hello Kitty explained that she was writing a speech for the devil. Suddenly there was belching. Hello Kitty chased after her evil energy, but couldn't catch it! Without her black edges, she could not remember what she wanted to say in her speech! Hello Kitty had been having trouble in the vortex, and now she was becoming *obsessed* with the passage of time. Then Hello Kitty brightened up. She knew so many sinister people. She could ask each of them what they thought about incomprehensible cruel things! Grandpa told Hello Kitty that there were porn actors, wet and naked, in the briefcase. Grandma added, today was a day for monstrous operations. Mama told Hello Kitty that shots of darkness were gradually becoming larger. Papa told Hello Kitty that ghosts' legs poked out and involved a bit of mischief. Mimmy told Hello Kitty that Corpses hijacked evil. Hello Kitty went home and found four well-groomed deaths. The next day Hello Kitty had her speech all ready. She talked about cursing and shivered. Everybody spewed and killed. It was time to celebrate! They had a big mocking party. Everyone laughed and cried. And before the day was over, they made sure to hurt each other, especially their sweet friend, Hello Kitty.

Hello Kitty's Gloom Room

One night, Hello Kitty noticed nerves swelling in the sky and she went outside to admire them. It was so ambiguous! As she looked up at the black curtain with all the faces, she thought about hell and the things her piece-of shit friends enjoyed. Hello Kitty wished for a brand-new tongue for Fifi. Jodie would like a new ball and breast. Thomas's organs were getting a bit rusty— he needed new ones. Hello Kitty wished for a shiny, psychic ghost for Tracy's bike. What about Dear Daniel? His wish had to be for something *really* eerie. What should she wish for? It was time for bed, but Hello Kitty had one last wish to make. The lucky star was clenching. Hello Kitty wished she could snort and slash suspended. That's it! A threat of death would be the perfect gift for Dear Daniel. After she got into bed, Hello Kitty drew a picture of her Gloom Room in her diary. She wrote down all the darkness and anxieties she had made for her friends. Mama came in to turn out the light. What was Hello Kitty writing about? Hello Kitty told Mama about the evil chill and stifled groans. Mama thought it was a great idea to look pale like you're dead already.

Grudge Trip

Hello Kitty enjoyed executions! One day at school, she stabbed a hideous fax machine. When Hello Kitty returned home from school, Mama appeared as a grotesque figure, and showed her an aroused demon she'd received in the mail. Hello Kitty had won a night of entwined limbs, some orgasm beers, and a trip to America. She invited her friends to come along. The first stop was New York City, where Hello Kitty and her friends survived on occult arts and cotton candy. Next up was Nantucket, where Hello Kitty admired the cuts and violent heavings. Then Florida, which was full of decay and menace. The next stop was Vermont, where there were enemies and erupting brains. Hawaii was last and where Hello Kitty learned how to play Russian Roulette and creep herself. When Hello Kitty arrived home, she told Mama and Mimmy that it was their time to die.

Virus Party

All week long, Hello Kitty couldn't wait for bubonic plague and to be ravaged by the Devil. Fifi was coming over for intense pain! The whole week at school Hello Kitty thought about what they would do in the Thick Woods Isolation Ward. Should they drip blood, perform surgeries, dig up remains? Finally the indiscriminate attack arrived. Hello Kitty woke up early and, with Mimmy's help, she picked up all her bones. When they were finished, they were very haunted! What should they do next? Hello Kitty, Fifi, and Mimmy decided to undulate in a ghastly shaft. Next, Fifi and Mimmy helped Hello Kitty mix agonising shrieks. Then they headed to the well, where they played *Watch the Bodies Slide into the Black Mouth*. After all this fun, everyone was hungry. Mama asked Mimmy and Hello Kitty to set the table for disease. Papa joined them right as the gaping wounds were ready. At the table, everyone discussed the murderous intent. What should they have for desperation? Mama suggested virus. Virus! Of course, a virus party was the best idea! At 3 o'clock, Fifi arrived with her infection and deep uncertainty. Hello Kitty got out the rope and darkness, and they all got melancholy.

Bones in the Garden

Early spring, when the days started getting black and a little twisted, Mama, Grandma, and Hello Kitty had a tradition. They started pulling bones out of the cold earth in the garden. Hello Kitty knew it was time to start coating everything with hatred and yellowish, brown scabs. Every year, sometime in the middle of April, she went down to the basement with Mama to find skulls and shadows. This year, Hello Kitty, Mama, and Grandma were going to plant curses, and nasty distorted faces. On the front lawn, they could grow piss plants! That didn't take any work at all. Hello Kitty thought they smelled great. The apocalyptic evil was going to take some extra work. Hello Kitty and Mama made tombs for them to wrap themselves around. Hello Kitty wanted to plant lots of dead insects around the garden, too. On the first day, Hello Kitty, Mama and Grandma did lots of crawling and dangling. You couldn't be afraid of the voices of insects if you wanted to be a devil. Lots of times you had to kneel down in the gooseflesh. Hello Kitty wanted to stay outside to see if death started breathing down her neck. Mimmy came outside to bear witness to the terror of the dream. Hello Kitty and Mimmy practised an endless, black, watery, underground game. After the game, it was time to go inside for groans and shudders. After they stuffed bones in plastic bags, it was time for bed. The next day after school, Hello Kitty raced home to check on her bottomless evil. Still nothing. She dutifully watered her seeds with spittle and blood. Saturday morning, she ran outside as soon as she woke up. It turned out that, during the days and nights when Hello Kitty didn't think anything was happening, the garden walls were closing in on all sides, leering at her: *there's no escape.*

Apocalypse Poems

1.

They wanted a similar campaign to Halloween & Valentine's Day,
but the theme and message weren't so clear. There were no red love
hearts or ghoulish faces, for the apocalypse. Nothingness was hard
to design, manufacture and, most importantly, sell, and they were
all out of catchy straplines.

2.

The bunkers came fully equipped with sex robots and cyanide
capsules. Although, potential buyers were a little nervous about the
former, in case of a *2001: A Space Odyssey* or *Jurassic Park* situation.
The bunkers came in a range of colours, had swimming pools, tennis
courts, interlinking 'playrooms', plastic jungles, karaoke bars and a
small chapel, where you could get married in the style of Hitler and
Eva Braun, by an Elvis impersonator, just 40 hours before
committing suicide.

3.

They decided to have an apocalypse ball. There was much
excitement in the village. What kind of punch would there be, what
type of pavlova? It was assumed that all attendees would have sex
with each other, indeed that it would become an orgy of heretofore
unimaginable depravity, given that long-term strategies and
commitment didn't matter any more. But then nor did money or
work experience, so 50% of those invited weren't able to secure
themselves a babysitter.

4.

Fabian's masturbation practice during lockdown reached a professional standard. He was becoming more supple and agile, his imagination was flourishing, colour constantly in his cheeks, and if he hadn't have lunged quite so deeply, one Sunday morning, incorporating his masturbation into his prayer and yoga rituals, if he hadn't overstretched so, and felt like he could really accomplish something, all his limbs would have been securely in their sockets for the earth's inevitable demise.

5.

Cheryl wanted to make up one more dance routine and perform it via Zoom to her hubby on death row before the world ended. The fact that her and her beau were now in the same situation, facing death, brought them closer together. She bought an orange prison jumpsuit and shot a traffic warden, to strengthen their connection further. However, she was regretting the former, due to her severe blushing issues and the consequential colour clash.

6.

If they could just come up with an absolute banger, something that really captured the ultimate *vibe* of the apocalypse, something that encapsulated what it was really about, that spoke to every person of every social standing, every religion and belief, then they would still be remembered by absolutely no-one.

7.

Jeff and Sandra had run out of things to say. They'd talked *about* the apocalypse, they'd talked *around* the apocalypse. They'd had sex to Eugene McDaniel's headless *Heroes of the Apocalypse* album in every room in the house. But now this was boring. So Sandra cut off Jeff's head, hollowed it out and used it for a lantern.

8.

As the lead-up to the apocalypse went on, Francine and Herbert became masters of the sourdough loaf and decided to bring it into their role-play, bring it into the bedroom and, inevitably, into the kitchen. But the flour was quite drying and after some initial friction-based issues, he set inside her, solid, and they died, just prior to the world ending.

9.

With the apocalypse coming the family decided to let go of their grudges. Many of which had run for decades. It all seemed so pointless now. So they decided to have a gathering: drinks, music and dancing, like the good ol' days when jealousy, failure and resentment weren't quite so rife amongst them. Sadly, on the evening, Barry mentioned something about Lenny's first wife's affair, a particular sore point. Lenny castrated him, Stevie stuck up for Barry by cutting off Lenny's ear, things escalated and they were all dead by morning.

10.

They heard the apocalypse was coming, but couldn't settle on what to wear. It had to be just right. Brian favoured a white and veiled set or one of his neon rompers. Janine was thinking bikini, but couldn't decide on the Bob Ross themed colour scheme, perhaps Titanium White, to match with Brian, or something from her bible characters range. They had a ritual planned, involving dunking, burning and a caterpillar breakdance, but wished the apocalypse could be a bit more specific about timings.

About The Author

Vik Shirley's pamphlet Corpses (Sublunary Editions) was published in 2020, her collection, *The Continued Closure of the Blue Door* (HVTN PRESS), was published in 2021, as was her book of photo-poetry *Disrupted Blue and Other Poems on Polaroid* (Hesterglock Press). Her work has appeared in such places as *Poetry London*, *The Rialto*, *Magma*, *Perverse*, *Shearsman* and *3am Magazine*. She is currently studying for a PhD in Dark Humour and the Surreal in Poetry at the University of Birmingham. Vik is Associate Editor of Sublunary Editions, editor of Surreal-Absurd at Mercurius Magazine, and tweets for Shearsman Books.

Acknowledgments

Many thanks to the editors of *Aww-Struck, Babel Tower Notice Board, Molly Bloom* and *Perverse*, where versions of some of these poems first appeared.

Thanks to Luke Palmer, Luke Kennard and Tom Jenks for their thoughts on this manuscript and to Richard Capener for his input on 'The Performance'. Thanks also to Kenz, Al, JP and Josh Rothes, for helping with some final decisions on cuts and versions.

Praise for the Author

"daniil kharms is a ghost on ecstasy as pianos mate with soup. what a horriful world shirley has made, it's almost as if life is silly and poetry is a space to affirm that."

- **SJ Fowler, poet who writes his own bios. Currently active www.stevenjfowler.com**

"Grotesque, like a Hieronymus Bosch footlong hotdog with Mark E Smith on onions."

- **Tom Jenks writes books, reads books and works tirelessly for a better Britain.**

"There's a little world in every poem here, uncannily our own and discombobulatingly other."

- **Luke Kennard is a poet and novelist who lectures at the University of Birmingham.**

L - #0717 - 100122 - C0 - 210/148/2 - PB - DID3244547